DATE DUE

FOLLETT

SUN

SOLAR SYSTEM

Lynda Sorensen

The Rourke Corporation, Inc.
Vero Beach, Florida 32964

Edited by Sandra A. Robinson

PHOTO CREDITS

© Lynn M. Stone: cover, title page, pages 4, 7, 12, 21;
© Hal Jandorf: page 18; courtesy of NASA: pages 8, 10, 13, 15, 17

Library of Congress Cataloging-in-Publication Data

Sorensen, Lynda, 1953-
 Sun / by Lynda Sorensen.
  p.   cm. — (The Solar system)
 Includes index.
 Summary: Illustrations and text present information about the features of the sun, solar activity and eclipses, and the importance of the sun to life on Earth.
  ISBN 0-86593-272-7
 1. Sun—Juvenile literature. [1. Sun.] I. Title. II. Series: Solar system (Vero Beach, Fla.)
 QB521.5.S67 1993
 523.7—dc20   93-14872
                                                        CIP
                                                        AC

Printed in the USA

TABLE OF CONTENTS

THE SUN

Our sun—that huge, glowing ball in the sky—is just one of billions of stars. The sun, however, looks bigger and brighter than other stars because it is much closer to Earth.

Like other stars, the sun is an extremely hot body of gas. No part of the sun is solid or liquid. The sun produces its own heat and light, called **solar** energy.

*The closest star—our sun,
a glowing ball in the sky*

THE SUN'S LIGHT

The sun's light takes about eight minutes and 20 seconds to travel the 93 million miles from sun to Earth. Light travels at a speed of about 186,000 miles per second!

All living things on Earth depend on sunlight for life. Plants change sunlight into food. Animals then eat the plants or other animals that have eaten plants.

Sunlight can cause eye damage and sunburn. Never look directly at the sun, and wear lotion for protection.

Plants change sunlight into food and provide the base of life on Earth

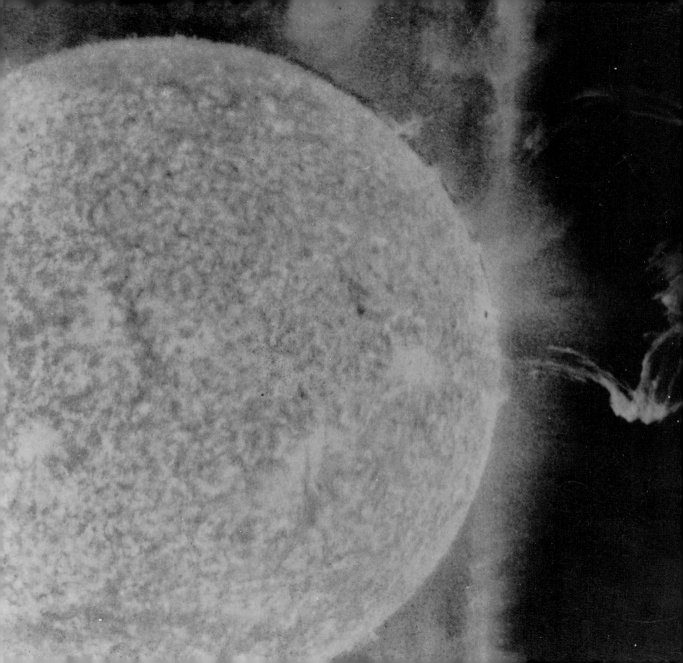

FEATURES OF THE SUN

The sun's churning mass is made of two main gases: hydrogen and helium. At the sun's center, these gases work together—during nuclear reactions—to produce incredible amounts of energy. This energy causes violent mixing motions that help "stir" the energy up to the surface of the sun.

The energy, in the form of heat and light, streams from the sun into space. Only a tiny amount of the sun's heat and light actually reaches Earth. The remainder is lost in space.

9

The sun is a mass of hot, churning gases

THE SUN AND PLANETS

Nine large, ball-shaped **planets** follow pathways in space around the sun. Our Earth is one of the planets. The planets, sun and many smaller objects in space make up our **solar system.**

Earth is the third closest planet to the sun. It gets exactly the right amount of heat and sunlight needed for life. The other planets seem to be too hot or cold for life.

The sun is at the center of our solar system

As the Earth turns, the sun sets in the west

A tongue of fire erupts from the sun in this image taken through a solar telescope

THE SUN AND EARTH

The sun could swallow the Earth many times over. The sun's mass is 330,000 times greater than Earth's.

The Earth travels around the sun in an oval path, or **orbit.** It takes 365 days—one year—for the Earth to complete a journey around the sun.

The Earth is held in orbit by the sun's strong **gravity.** Gravity is a powerful, invisible natural force that holds things in place.

Planet Earth travels around the sun in an orbit

SOLAR ACTIVITY

The sun's surface is constantly changing. Solar flares are one type of solar activity. These are great bursts of light caused by the release of large amounts of energy.

Solar storms and sunspots are two other types of solar activity. Sunspots are dark, round blotches on the sun. The cooler gases in a sunspot shine less brightly than warmer gases, so sunspots appear dark.

Solar activity sometimes affects radio signals and weather on Earth.

A spectacular solar flare spans 367,000 miles across the sun's surface

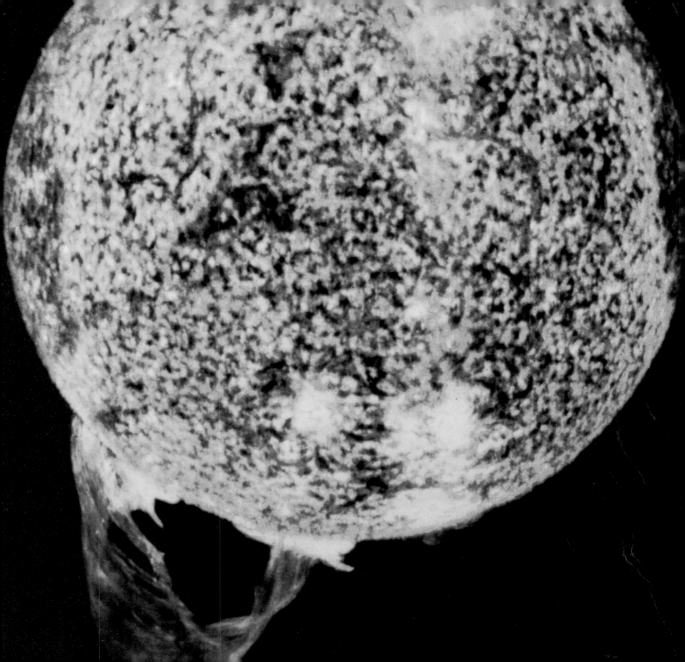

A SOLAR ECLIPSE

The moon travels in an orbit around the Earth. Every so often, the moon's path takes it directly between the sun and Earth. In that position, the moon blocks the sun's light to Earth, causing brief darkness during the day. This is called a **solar eclipse.**

An eclipse lasts only a few minutes because the moon keeps moving.

A solar eclipse photographed in 1979

DAYS, NIGHTS AND SEASONS

The Earth spins, or rotates, daily as it orbits the sun. The side of the Earth that faces the sun has daylight, and the dark side has night. As the Earth turns, day fades into night and then night brightens into day.

The Earth's angle toward the sun changes, and this changes our seasons. When Earth's northern half tilts toward the sun, it receives more of the sun's direct heat and light. Then North America enjoys summer. When Earth's southern pole tilts toward the sun, South America has summer and North America has winter.

When Earth's south pole tilts toward the sun, North America enjoys winter

STUDYING THE SUN

Astronomers are scientists who study the sun, moon, stars, planets and other heavenly bodies. Astronomers use special equipment such as solar **telescopes** to study the sun and its light.

The solar telescope helps astronomers learn more about what the sun and other stars are like. Scientists are also studying ways to collect and use the sun's heat and light, or solar energy.

Glossary

astronomer (uh STRON uh mer) — a scientist who studies the sun, moon, stars and other heavenly bodies

gravity (GRAHV ih tee) — a powerful, invisible natural force that holds things in place

orbit (OR bit) — the path that an object follows as it repeatedly travels around an object in space

planet (PLAN it) — any one of the nine large, ball-shaped heavenly bodies that orbit the sun

solar (SO ler) — having to do with the sun

solar eclipse (SO ler ee KLIPS) — a situation in which the moon's path briefly blocks the light from the sun

solar system (SO ler SIS tim) — the sun, planets, and other heavenly bodies that revolve around the sun

telescope (TEL ess kope) — a powerful instrument used to magnify and view distant objects

INDEX